The Library of
NATIVE AMERICANS™

The Modoc
of California and Oregon

Jack S. Williams

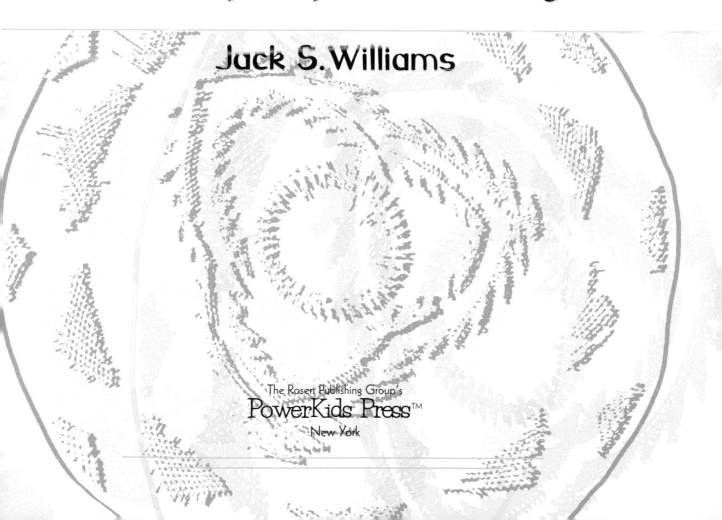

The Rosen Publishing Group's
PowerKids Press™
New York

For my friend, Abel Silvas, who never forgot the meaning of standing by his ancestors

Published in 2004 by The Rosen Publishing Group, Inc.
29 East 21st Street, New York, NY 10010

Cover, p. 33 © Tom Bean/Corbis; pp. 6, 50 (left) Library of Congress Prints and Photographs Division; pp. 7, 50 (right) Lava Beds National Monument; pp. 10, 26 courtesy of the Phoebe Apperson Hearst Museum of Anthropology and the Regents of the University of California; p. 12 © Joseph Van Os/The Image Bank; p. 13 © Stuart Westmorland/The Image Bank; p. 14 Eastman's Originals Collection, Department of Special Collections, General Library, University of California, Davis; pp. 16, 30 courtesy of the C. Hart Merriam Collection of Native American Photographs, The Bancroft Library, University of California, Berkeley; pp. 19, 23, 25 National Anthropological Archives, Smithsonian Institution, INV # 0157800; pp. 21, 28 INV # 0160404102, INV # 09837300 National Anthropological Archives, Smithsonian Institution; p. 34 from *Handbook of the Indians of California*, California Book Company, A. L. Kroeber, Berkeley, CA,1953; p. 36 Harvey Spector Photography/Turtle Bay Exploration Park; p. 38 drawing by Father Ignacio Tirsch, courtesy of the National Library of the Czech Republic; pp. 40, 43 courtesy of Seaver Center for Western History Research, Natural History Museum of Los Angeles; p. 45 National Anthropological Archives, Smithsonian Institution, INV # 01604204; pp. 47 (X-32459), 48 (X-32143), 53 (X-32460) Western History Collection/Denver Public Library; p. 49 © Corbis; pp. 54, 57 © Mark E. Gibson at CLM/Corbis; p. 56 © AP/Wide World Photos.

Designer: Geri Fletcher; Editor: Charles Hofer; Photo Researcher: Sherri Liberman

Williams, Jack S.
The Modoc of California and Oregon / Jack S. Williams.— 1st ed.
        p. cm. — (The library of Native Americans)
Summary: Describes the culture, government, arts, and religion of the Modoc people of California and Oregon. Includes bibliographical references and index.
ISBN 1-4042-2660-5 (lib. bdg.)
1. Modoc Indians—History—Juvenile literature. 2. Modoc Indians—Social life and customs—Juvenile literature. [1. Modoc Indians. 2. Indians of North America—Oregon. 3. Indians of North America—California.] I. Title. II. Series.
E99.M7W55 2004
979.4004'974122—dc22
                                                                    2003015143

Manufactured in the United States of America

On the cover: A woven Modoc basket.

A variety of terminologies has been employed in works about Native Americans. There are sometimes differences between the original names or terms used by a Native American group and the anglicized or modernized versions of such names or terms. Although this book contains terms that we feel will be most recognizable to our readership, there may also exist synonymous or native words that are preferred by certain speakers.

Contents

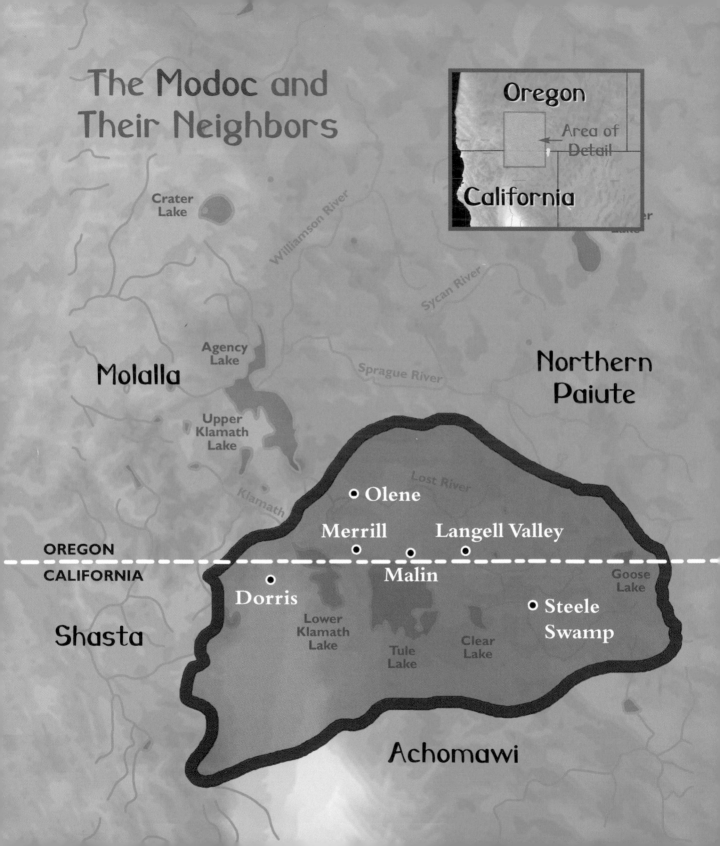

The Modoc and Their Neighbors

Oregon

Area of Detail

California

Crater Lake

Williamson River

Sycan River

Molalla

Agency Lake

Sprague River

Northern Paiute

Upper Klamath Lake

Klamath

Lost River

○ Olene

Merrill
○

Langell Valley
○

OREGON

CALIFORNIA

Malin
○

Goose Lake

○ Dorris

Lower Klamath Lake

○ Steele Swamp

Shasta

Tule Lake

Clear Lake

Achomawi

One

Introducing the Modoc People

The border of northeastern California and Oregon is a land of black volcanic plateaus covered by sagebrush and pine forests. This part of America is located far away from large western cities, like San Francisco, California, and Portland, Oregon. Here, there are few places that are well known to tourists or other outsiders. Each year, 12 to 16 inches (30.5 to 40.6 centimeters) of rain and snow fall in the area. The water collects in rushing rivers, vast marshes, and peaceful lakes. Among the most important bodies of water are Lower Klamath Lake, Tule Lake, and Clear Lake. This peaceful countryside is also a place where the temperature changes dramatically during the year. The frozen days of January average a mere 16°F (-9°C). By contrast, the summers are extremely hot. During July, the temperature often climbs above 85°F (30°C). For thousands of years, this land was the home of the Modoc Nation. These people are the focus of this book.

No one is certain where the name "Modoc" came from. Some experts believe that it started out as a word used by the Kalapuya people, a neighboring native nation, to identify the Modoc. Others note both the Klamath (also spelled "Klammath") and the Modoc use the word "Maklak" for themselves. This term simply means "the

This map details the Modoc territory in California and Oregon.

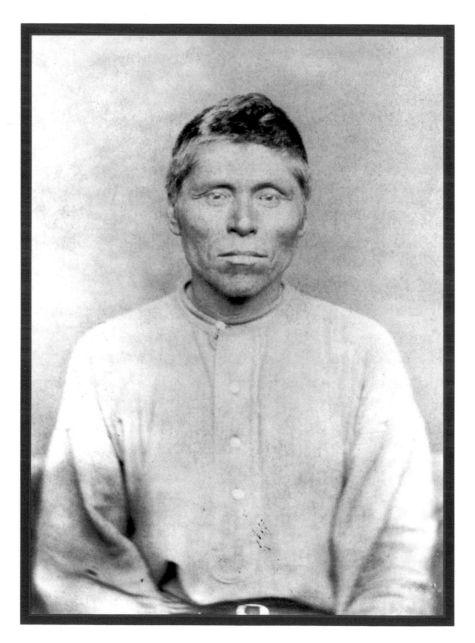

6 Over the centuries, the Modoc culture would go through many changes. This portrait of a Modoc doctor, taken in the late nineteenth century, shows how certain clothing was adopted from the newcomers.

people." Some think the word "Modoc" was the closest that the English-speaking settlers could get to "Maklak."

When the first citizens of the United States arrived in the region around 1850, there was a total of between 600 and 800 Modoc people. The Modoc divided their nation into three major groups based on where they lived during the winter. These were the Gombatwas, or Lower Klamath Lake people, the Gogewas, or Lower Lost River people, and the Pasganwas, or Tule Lake people. Each group's hunting and gathering areas extended far to the south, east, and west. If a person asked Native Americans who they were, they usually gave their names and the name of their settlement.

Origins

The story of the first people who came to the land that would one day be called America is filled with many mysteries. Archaeologists study the objects that were left behind by people who lived in the

Pictographs, like the one pictured above, were a sacred part of the Modoc culture. This form of art was created by Modoc who painted on rock formations.

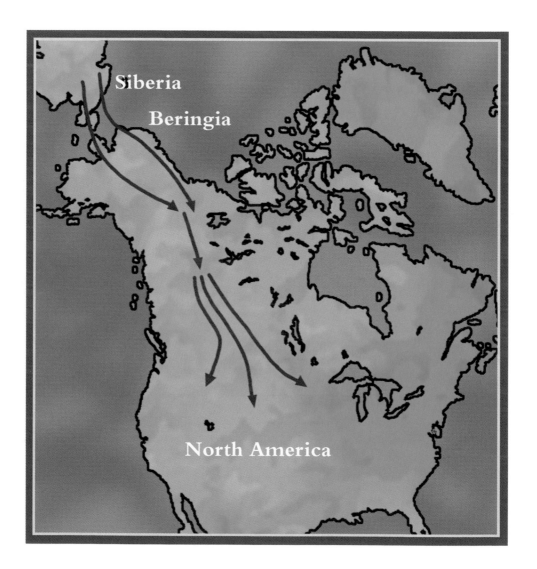

Siberia

Beringia

North America

8   This map details the routes taken by tribes crossing the Bering Strait. The strait was once covered with land and ice, making the crossing possible. Today it is a series of small islands between Alaska and Russia.

past. Their studies suggest that the first Native Americans came from Asia sometime between 13,000 and 40,000 years ago by crossing over a land bridge, a series of frozen bridges that connected north-eastern Russia with what is today Alaska. These Asian tribes were probably following large herds of animals that traveled between the two continents. Once they had reached the region of Alaska, the people moved south, following the migrating herds. Within less than a thousand years, some of the continent's first people had reached the tip of South America.

The ancestors of the Modoc were among the people who made this amazing journey. However, they were probably not the first Native Americans to live along the California-Oregon border. The first people in this region were probably the ancestors of the modern Hokan speakers, such as the neighboring Shasta Nation. The Modoc speak a language that comes from the Lutuamian family. Their ancestors probably arrived between 4,000 and 6,000 years ago. The researchers who study this period are not sure if the Modoc moved in peacefully, or if they fought their way in as part of an invasion.

Experts who study Native Americans still have many questions about the story of the early Modoc people. There have not been many archaeological excavations in their territories. Many modern Native Americans disagree with what the archaeologists have put together in regards to their history. The Native Americans insist their ancestors always existed in their traditional homelands, since the time that they first appeared on Earth.

Two
Daily Life

The first Europeans who entered the Modoc country found Native Americans who had a very different kind of lifestyle than they were used to. The Europeans thought that they were better than the Modoc, who they saw as primitive people. Although they did not do certain things the way that the newcomers did, the Modoc had an amazing ability to live in close cooperation with the natural world. Today, researchers and other outsiders are coming to appreciate the Modoc way of life. They recognize that many of the Modoc's views were more advanced than those of the Europeans.

Living off the Land

The Modoc lived in a world dominated by marshes, sagebrush, and forests. They acquired nearly everything they needed from hunting and gathering. Unlike many other native peoples, the Modoc did not grow crops. Although the land was rugged, it had many resources.

The Modoc territory was filled with useful animals. The streams, marshes, and lakes were teeming with fish, beavers, otters, and turtles.

These two Modoc women pose for a photograph at the Klamath Reservation in the early twentieth century. After newcomers moved in and claimed much of its land, the Modoc world was reduced to small reservations.

There were hundreds of types of water birds, including ducks, geese, pelicans, and swans. The land was filled with pronghorn antelopes, elk, bighorn sheep, grizzly bears, deer, wolves, coyotes, and dozens of other types of large animals. The Modoc country was also a place where a person could find thousands of varieties of smaller land creatures, such as snakes, lizards, rabbits, and insects. Nearly every wild animal that the land and waters supported had some useful place in the Modoc world.

The Modoc had only one kind of tamed animal. Like most other native peoples, they kept dogs as pets. These creatures guarded their settlements and helped the men when they went hunting.

The Modoc lived in close relationship with wildlife. Magnificent creatures like this bighorn sheep played an important role in Modoc life.

The plants of the Modoc territory also provided important resources. The natives made extensive use of reeds and bulrushes for dozens of different kinds of items, including boats, housing, food, and clothing. The shorelines of the streams and lakes were the homes of hundreds of other kinds of edible plants. The pine trees were transformed into building materials. They also produced spiny cones. When these seed pods were roasted, they gave up delicious pine nuts. Throughout the landscape there were many kinds of flavorful wild fruits, including wild plums, wild grapes, and chokecherries. Many of the other plants of the Modoc homeland were used as medicines.

Bears were a feared and respected part of the Modoc region.

14   This photograph captures the beauty of Clear Lake in the Modoc territory. The land of the Modoc offered plenty of natural resources abundant in plant and animal life.

The changing seasons saw the Modoc move from one abundant food resource to the next. The springtime was filled with fishing when fish were more active in the Modoc waters. The warm and sunny days of summer were a time of hunting in the mountains. During the fall, many different types of plants became ripe, and the Modoc spent much of their time gathering. During the fiercely cold winters, the Modoc returned to their permanent winter villages. During this season everyone depended on the foods they had stored earlier in the year.

Villages

The Modoc had two kinds of villages. Their permanent homes were located along the major waterways and lakes. Here, they spent the winter in larger wood and earth lodges. During the other seasons, most of the people lived in temporary settlements that were made up of huts. These villages were moved to different hunting and gathering areas according to the availability of wild foods.

When the Europeans arrived in the Modoc country during the early 1800s, they found around thirty villages. The population size of each settlement ranged between ten and fifty individuals.

The Modoc's territory was divided into clear sections through a complex system of ownership. Each winter village had its own larger territory. The population owned the right to hunt, fish, and gather in this area. Any person from the outside had to get permission to use the village lands. If someone was found in the region without permission, he or she was viewed as a thief and might be attacked or even killed.

The Modoc built two basic types of houses. The winter homes were built inside pits that measured 3 to 4 feet (0.9 to 1.2 meters) deep. They had round floor plans, and the walls were made of thick wooden planks. The roof beams supported a layer of grass,

This photograph shows the ruins of a Modoc sweat house. The sweat houses served many different purposes in Modoc culture.

or mats, and the entire structure was covered with earth. The entranceway to the home was a round hole in the roof. In order to come into the house, you had to climb down a pole-like ladder. This ladder had toe holes cut into its surface to make it easier to climb. The roof entrance allowed sunlight to enter and smoke from cooking and heating fires to escape. Most of the homes measured between 10 and 20 feet (3 to 6.1 m) in diameter.

Some of the big structures were used as village assembly halls. Inside these buildings the people would come together to perform rituals and hold community dances. The Modoc called their assembly halls kshiulgish.

A second type of home was used by the Modoc in their temporary villages. It was made out of willow poles and brush or reeds. These huts had a rectangular or oval floor plan. The corners of the rectangular buildings were almost always rounded off. The huts ranged in length from 12 to 25 feet (3.7 to 7.6 m). They were usually about half as wide as they were long. Willow poles were set into the ground and then tied together to create a framework for the covering. A long ridge pole ran down the center of the roof. Three layers of mats or reeds usually served as the outer walls.

Most of the Modoc communities built sweat houses to take steam baths. Some of these buildings were small. These structures were assembled inside shallow pits. Willow poles were bent over to form a dome-shaped framework. The outer surface was covered with mud, reed mats, or skins. Outside the hut, the Modoc started a fire in a pit surrounded by rocks. In order to use the bath, the Modoc moved the hot rocks to a small hole in the ground, located at the back end of the hut. Water was sprinkled on the rocks to create steam. A few of the Modoc communities had a second kind of larger sweat house. These structures were probably similar to the Modoc's winter homes. The bathers would usually spend only a short time in the steam of the sweat house. They would then jump into the cold waters of a nearby stream or lake to cool off from the intense heat of the sweat house. The men took baths for recreation, for religious purposes, and for their health. The Modoc called these baths spuklish.

Cooking

The women usually prepared the meals. The native cooks used a wide variety of techniques to prepare their dishes. The foods were very different from those eaten by most modern Americans. However, to the Modoc they were both nutritious and delicious.

The Modoc ground some of their food into flour using a special volcanic stone that looked like a bowl. This device is known as a metate. The Modoc's metates were specially designed to process delicate foods. They were different from those used by most other Native Americans. The Modoc metates had two large horn-like bumps to allow the person to grind the food by hand. The user carefully pressed the materials being ground into the volcanic metate using her hands. Most metates that were popular with other native nations were used along with a hand-grinding stone. The many different types of flour could be combined with water to make a tasty soup or roasted as flat cakes.

The Modoc used tightly woven baskets to prepare liquid foods, like stews and soups. The cooks heated small stones, which were mixed with the food inside a basket. They had to keep stirring the liquid or the stones would burn a hole in the woven basket. By replacing the hot stones several times, water could even be boiled. The Modoc used a similar technique to roast insects on basket trays. Other small items could be heated by setting them down on stones that surrounded a fire pit.

The Modoc chefs also cooked in earthen ovens. The first thing they did was dig a hole 2 or 3 feet (0.6–0.9 m) into the ground. A large fire was started in the pit.

Winnowing trays like these were used to sift flour during food preparation. These trays were woven by expert Modoc craftspeople.

Meanwhile, the cooks wrapped meat or whatever they were cooking in leaves. When the fire had burned down, the fuel was removed using large sticks. The wrapped packages of food were placed in the pit and covered by rocks or soil. A few hours later, the food was excavated, or dug up. The packages were opened, and their contents were ready to eat.

Most of the fish and meat that was brought to the village ended up being preserved by smoking. The women cut the meat from animals and fish into long strips. The thin pieces were draped over a wooden rack as a small fire burned below. After a few hours, the smoked meat could be removed and stored or ground into flour.

Clothing and Body Decoration

The Modoc wore clothing that was well suited to the extremes in weather they experienced each year. Men and women had shirts, moccasins, and many different kinds of belts. Nearly everyone used one or more bags suspended from their waists or shoulders. Most adults also wore small caps or hats. The women wore skirts and several types of longer gowns. When the winter came, blankets, capes, and heavy robes were popular. The native craftspeople also created snowshoes.

Most Modoc had clothes made from deerskin. The outfits of the wealthy natives were often assembled from the more valued elk, bobcat, and mountain lion skins. The poorer people often wore garments made from the less desirable rabbit or bird skins.

This is a portrait of Shar-Kah, also known as Captain George, who was a member of the Warm Springs Tanino Nation in Washington State. He served as a scout for the United States Army during the Modoc War in the late nineteenth century.

21

Everyone made use of lighter forms of summer clothing that were made from reeds.

Ceremonial equipment included special feather headdresses, collars, and beaded garments. Woodpecker scalps, which had brightly colored feathers, were often used in clothing worn during religious ceremonies.

Like most other Native Americans, both Modoc men and women wore jewelry. Popular forms included beads, pendants, necklaces, bracelets, and earrings. These items were made from seashells, bones, feathers, and wood. Some especially beautiful examples were worn at religious ceremonies, although most Modoc jewelry was used as part of the natives' everyday clothing. After the arrival of Europeans, the Native Americans adopted many kinds of glass beads. Small beads were often sewn onto clothing. Other varieties were combined with shells and worn as bracelets or necklaces.

Flattened heads were considered to be beautiful. In order to achieve the desired head shape, the Modoc tied the head of a baby to a wooden cradle board to alter the shape of his or her skull. This kind of modification is called cranial deformation. Similar techniques were used by many different peoples throughout the world to change the shape of their babies' heads.

Cleanliness was very important to the Modoc. They frequently took baths in nearby lakes, rivers, and streams. They believed that this helped them to stay healthy and made them look more attractive.

Arts and Crafts

The Modoc people transformed things they found in the natural world into dozens of different kinds of beautiful and useful objects. These items are still valued by experts as examples of human ingenuity, skill, and artistry.

The Modoc men usually made the community's stone tools. They showed incredible skill in the ways they fashioned these objects

Modoc women were usually responsible for making baskets. These beautiful baskets had many practical purposes. They could also be traded for other goods.

using their bare hands. Many of the items they produced were made by chipping. The obsidian that was found in the region was an especially sharp kind of volcanic glass. It was probably the best raw material that could be found to fashion chipped stone objects. The natives' stonework included arrowheads, drills, spearheads, scrapers, and knives.

A second group of stone tools was made by grinding. Granite and sandstone were rubbed against harder rocks to manufacture pestles and metates used for preparing food. The Modoc also created weights for fishing nets by rubbing notches into smaller stones. Arrow shaft straighteners were made using a similar technique. Some stones were ground into small, bowl-like lamps that burned salmon oil as fuel. Smaller stones were also ground out to create L-shaped bowls. These devices were combined with hollow wooden stems to be used as smoking pipes.

The Modoc women made baskets from reeds, tree shoots, rushes, and grasses. These basket materials were also used to make

> Many of the items they produced were made by chipping. The obsidian that was found in the region was an especially sharp kind of volcanic glass. It was probably the best raw material that could be found to fashion chipped stone objects.

bowls, jars, trays, boxes, and fans. The women alternated the raw materials to produce geometric patterns.

The plants that were found in the Modoc's environment were the source of many other important materials. Besides cooking, wood was also used to make digging sticks, house poles, arrow shafts, spears, spoons, bowls, cups, and trays. Reeds were one of the most important types of raw material. They were used to make mats, house coverings, moccasins, leggings, cradles, and blankets.

Besides baskets the Modoc crafted many other practical household items such as this seed beater.

The Modoc of California and Oregon

The Modoc men created powerful bows from a combination of wood and deer muscle, or sinew. This kind of weapon, called a composite bow, is much more powerful than those that are just made out of wood. The native craftsmen fashioned arrows from a combination of feathers, wood, and reeds.

The animals of the Modoc country were used to make objects that served many other purposes. Sinew, skin, and fur were made into clothing, bedding, bags, and drums. Deer hooves were tied together to create rattles. Both animal and human hair were twisted together to make cords. The horns and bones of many different

Pine nuts were an abundant resource in the Modoc world. They were used for many different things, including jewelry, like this pine nut necklace.

creatures became scrapers, hair pins, fishhooks, jewelry, needles, awls, game equipment, and combs. The larger leg bones of deer and elk were used as hammers. Bird feathers were also used to create beautiful headdresses, arrows, clothing, and jewelry.

The Modoc were famous boat builders. They created canoes by digging out the centers of pine, cedar, or fir logs. These boats measured a little more than 2 feet wide (0.6 m) and came in lengths of 12, 20, or 30 feet (3.7, 6.1, or 9.1 m). When the craftsmen were finished, the sides were remarkably thin. The thirty-footers could hold up to five people. The Modocs called their log canoes vunsh. A second type of boat was created by tying together thick bundles of reeds. These vessels could be built up to a length of 15 feet (4.6 m). The reed canoes could hold only one or two people. The Modoc called these boats vunshaga.

Trade

The Modoc acquired some of the things they used through trade. They purchased slaves, beads, axes, fishhooks, several kinds of baskets, and blankets from the Klamath to their north. They traded with the Achumawi people to their south for bows, furs, and seashells. The Shasta people offered deerskin dresses and shirts. Other native nations provided feather blankets, axes, and wooden war clubs. In exchange for these goods, the Modoc offered shell beads, baskets, skirts, slaves, and hides. Like many other groups that lived in this region, the Modoc traders used shell beads as money.

Three

Other Aspects of Modoc Life

Social structure identifies how a society is divided into different groups. Every community, including those created by the Modoc, has a social structure. In Modoc society, people were assigned to a group based on whether they were men or women, where they lived, their wealth, their age, and who their parents were.

The family was the smallest Modoc social group. The eldest male was usually placed in charge of his relatives. The men took most of the responsibility for bringing in the larger game and fish. The women and children worked hard to gather plants and smaller animals. Some chiefs and wealthy men had more than one wife. Most marriages were arranged by older relatives. Both husbands and wives were expected to give gifts to their spouse's family at weddings. The men usually moved in with their wives until a few children were born. The new family then went to live in their own house.

A few families had more possessions than others. These wealthy people enjoyed the best quality of life in the Modoc villages. There were many more average families and some that could be considered poor. The wealthy Modoc families even owned slaves. These slaves had few rights and had to work for

Many photographers and artists portrayed the Native Americans as uncivilized and savage people. This photograph was most likely staged by the photographer to reinforce these ideas.

their masters without pay. Most were from the Achumawi and Atsugewi Nations and were captured in war.

One or more Modoc families formed a village. Every such community had a leader, or chief. The Modoc name for these men was lagi. This title was usually inherited from a person's parents. Sometimes doctors or religious leaders became lagi. Most of the chiefs came from wealthy families.

This photograph, taken in the 1870s, shows several Modoc women in dress typical of the time period.

The older people of the community often formed a special council of advisors. Most villages also had a number of doctors and other religious leaders. These people were always given special respect. They were believed to have powers over many unseen forces. Average villagers were afraid that the doctors might use their abilities to hurt them. The doctors were usually paid when they visited a sick person.

Government

The Modoc Nation never had a single tribal council, or government. Although they did not think of themselves as a unified political group, the Modoc did have a strong sense of identity that they shared amongst themselves. When it came to outside interference, they often helped each other.

Every Modoc community had a village chief. He was expected to settle any fights or disagreements that took place between families or individuals. The chief also helped to solve the community's problems when there was a crisis, such as a war or a drought. Most of the leaders were helped by a council of advisors. Several village chiefs occasionally formed a temporary alliance. However, these groups usually broke up when a war or conflict came to an end.

The Modoc gave special gifts to their chiefs. The leaders were expected to share their food and other property during shortages. The villagers felt that everyone in the community had the same basic rights and privileges. Even the leaders had to follow rules. The family was the only group in which someone could give direct orders. In all other matters, the people had some say in what they did. They usually went along with the things they felt were right and ignored anything they considered foolish or immoral.

Warfare

The Modoc men were famous warriors. They fought for many different reasons. Some struggles began when an individual from one settlement killed a person from another. Every Modoc warrior was quick to demand justice, and this meant getting even. Sometimes the people would turn to war when they thought a doctor from a rival village had used his supernatural powers against them. The wars could also start because someone wanted to get rich or become famous. Captured enemy women and children became slaves that could be sold or forced to work for the victors. Some warriors wanted to fight because they simply believed it was an important part of their lives.

The Modoc had many enemies, including the Achumawi, Klamath, and the Shasta peoples. Almost every year, several Modoc villages formed an alliance against the Shasta. During the summer, the warriors headed out to raid the Shasta settlements. Their enemies formed similar raiding parties and attacked the Modoc homeland. Some wars were also fought between rival Modoc villages.

The Modoc usually formed groups of ten to twenty warriors when they went on an expedition against their enemies. They were experts in catching their enemies off-guard in ambushes. Many of the raids were undertaken at night.

The Modoc's traditional weapons included bows and arrows, daggers, and spears. The spear was relatively short in length and used with an underhand thrust. It was almost never thrown at the enemy. A few warriors carried wooden clubs. After firearms and horses were introduced around 1850, the Modoc used them in both hunting and warfare. When the raiders were planning an attack along a waterway, they often used reed boats. These vessels could not be sunk and were very easy to maneuver.

Weapons like arrowheads and spearheads were made from chipped obsidian, a volcanic glass found throughout the Modoc region. This obsidian arrowhead was left behind in the Modoc's California homeland.

The Modoc's armor included elk hide helmets and shirts. These were sewn in a double thickness. Some of the elk shirts were reinforced with wooden rods. These modifications made the armor stronger. After guns were introduced, the Modoc's body defenses were no longer valuable. As a result, they gradually abandoned their use.

Hunting and Fishing

The Modoc men used many different techniques to hunt and fish. Every expedition began with elaborate prayers and rituals. The work of the hunter was a sacred duty, and there were many special rules for anyone who wanted to be included.

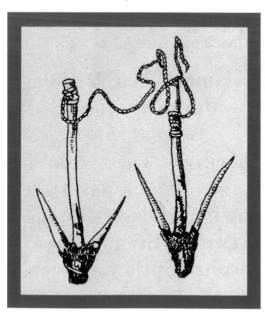

The Modoc's main weapon was their powerful composite bow. Some hunters used bolas to bring down birds and smaller creatures. These devices were made of stones tied to long pieces of leather. The user would twirl the bolas like a sling, and then release the device. The animals' legs, or wings, would become entangled in the flying bolas. The Modoc also used several different kinds of traps to drive larger animals, such as elk, into places where they were easier to kill. When they were hunting deer, the natives wore special headdresses

This illustration shows the design of fishhooks used by Modoc fishermen.

that were decorated with stuffed deer heads. These devices helped the natives to sneak up on the animals in the tall grass without being detected. Ducks and other waterfowl were ensnared using large nets. Other kinds of small animals were captured using nets, baskets, or rope traps. The community's dogs usually accompanied the men on hunts.

The native fishermen also relied on many different tools. Some of the water creatures were killed with spears or double-ended harpoons. The Modoc also used special fishing baskets and nets. In calm water, hooks and lines were extended into the water to capture the day's catch.

Language

The Modoc spoke a variety of language from the Lutuamian family. Some experts have classified them as part of the larger Penutian-speaking community. They shared their language with the nearby Klamath Nation that lived in Oregon. Although both the Modoc and Klamath had their own dialect, or language variety, speakers from either group could be easily understood by each other.

Religion

The Modoc Nation had its own religion. The elders taught every community member the things they needed to know about God and what it took to be a good person. They taught the people that many of the things they saw in the world around them had spirits. The

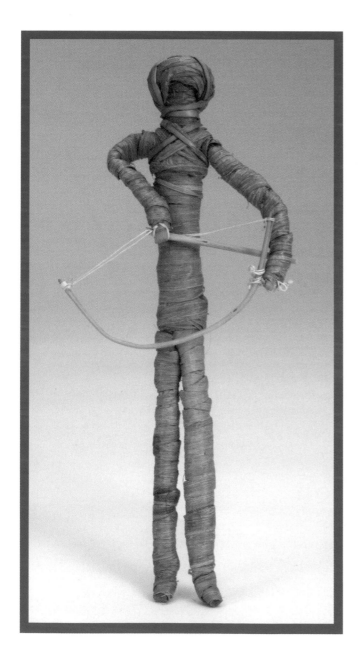

Modoc were also responsible for completing many public and private rituals. It was not easy for a person to live up to the high standards required to be a good Modoc.

As an individual grew older, he or she celebrated many special rituals. Every young person enjoyed a ceremony when becoming an adult. There were also extravagant marriages. The end of a person's life was marked by an elaborate funeral when the body was burned. A person's spirit went off to no-lisg-ni, a place that existed beyond the mountains to the west. The elders made it clear that you had to avoid certain foods and places during the ritual periods. Many ceremonies required visits to the sweat houses.

The Modoc elders taught many of their most important

36 Not everything the Modoc made had strict practical purposes. This is a photo of a Modoc doll.

religious ideas using stories. For example, some old people told of Kmukamch (or Gmukamps). This ancient man created the people who inhabited the earth. He was also the master of many tricks. When there was an earthquake, the children were told that it was only Kmukamch shaking the earth.

The Modoc's doctors' work also involved religion. In order to be effective, they had to understand the spirits of many unseen powers. Modoc villagers often became ill because they believed these supernatural energies were not being controlled. Some sick people died unless a doctor gave them the right treatment.

Whenever people came together to celebrate a religious holiday, they played gambling games. Some of these amusements used short wooden sticks as counters. A ring and pin toy was made out of reeds. The public rituals often included songs that were performed using rattles, hide drums, and bone flutes.

The Modoc created many different symbols, or signs, by scratching into or painting rocky places. The images that were painted are called pictographs. The designs that were scratched into the rock are called petroglyphs. No one is certain why the Modoc created this rock art. Some experts believe that they were made during rituals. Because all forms of rock art are sacred to many modern Native Americans, it is essential that everyone show respect when viewing it.

Four

Dealing with the Newcomers

European explorers reached the coastline of northern California in 1542. A series of voyages of discovery followed. By 1650, both Spain and England claimed the western edge of North America, including the mountains and valleys that stretched into the interior. However, the Europeans did little to explore or colonize this immense region. The Modoc continued their lives much as they had during the previous centuries.

Some of the events that were taking place beyond the horizon did have consequences for the Modoc. The Europeans inadvertently brought terrible diseases to the Americas. Illnesses like measles and smallpox probably killed many Modocs. In other parts of North America, these diseases caused the early deaths of up to 90 percent of the population. Since the Native Americans had not been exposed to the diseases before, they easily fell victim. Many historians believe Euopeans sometimes purposefully spread smallpox to Native Americans by giving them blankets infected with the disease. This way the Native Americans were weakened, and the Europeans moved in to claim their land. Unfortunately, we do not have written accounts that describe what happened to the natives of the interior of California and Oregon. As a result, we will probably never know

This illustration captures a Spanish settlement along the coast of Baja California in Mexico. As the Europeans extended their control to the north, they brought many drastic changes to the Modoc way of life.

how many people died. However, most experts agree that the new diseases claimed many victims.

The Modoc and Outsiders, 1769–1850

Between 1769 and 1850, many different foreign nations claimed the Modoc country. The Spaniards, British, Mexicans, Russians, and people from the United States all maintained that they had the right to rule California and Oregon. During this entire period, the Modoc people never even saw any invading soldiers. But they undoubtedly heard some stories about the strangers' activities in regions to the

The California gold rush, which began in 1849, would forever change the landscape of the Modoc territory. Newcomers seeking riches would eventually force the Modoc off their own land.

south and west. They knew that there were problems with the newcomers. However, the fighting and changes mostly seemed far away. The Modoc were safe.

The first foreigners who actually explored the Modoc region did not arrive until after 1820. These intruders came to trade and trap, not to take over the land. The fur trappers and mountain men wanted animal skins they could sell in the Far East, Europe, and the distant settlements of the United States. Most of the foreigners came from British and United States settlements located on the coast of modern Washington and Oregon. They soon discovered that the Modoc country contained few of the animals that they were interested in. As a result, they did not focus much of their efforts on the region.

By the time the United States conquered California in 1847, the outsiders' trade goods had begun to play an important part in Modoc life. The natives loved glass beads. They were incorporated into nearly all classes of jewelry and clothing decoration. The Modoc quickly discovered that iron and steel tools were superior to those made from stone or bone. Still, prior to 1850, European trade items were never plentiful. The Modoc lived far away from any trading post, and they had to rely on exchanges with other Native American nations for these goods.

The year 1848 was a turning point in the history of the entire western United States. The discovery of gold near Sacramento brought tens of thousands of foreigners into California. The newcomers' search for precious metal quickly expanded into Modoc territory. Nearly all of the miners believed that Native Americans were backward and ugly. To them, the natives were simply an enemy that had to be killed or pushed away. They hated the Modoc although the natives had done nothing to them. During the next fifty years, the Modoc Nation was thrown into a time of horror. The discovery of gold that made some men millionaires unlocked unbelievable devastation for the native peoples.

The Modoc Versus the European Invaders, 1848–1900

The miners soon established camps and towns in the territory to the west of the Modoc. Settlers immediately began to slaughter the Native Americans who lived close to their diggings. In 1849, the invaders created a trail that passed right through the center of the Modoc's homeland. The people who traveled on this highway hunted animals without permission and drove away many others. The newcomers justified their actions by saying that the Modoc and other natives had no rights and were not really human beings.

Many American political leaders agreed with the miners who feared and hated the Modoc. Governor Peter H. Burnett of California wrote that he looked forward to the complete destruction of every Native American nation in the region. The men who served as judges told the invading miners and ranch owners that they had the right to make Indian children serve as slaves and that they should force the adults to do whatever they wanted. Some of the government officials and people who lived in the eastern United States did not agree with these policies. They wanted to find some kind of arrangement that would allow the miners to work freely while still protecting the native peoples.

For the time being, the Modoc had no interest in talking peace with any outsiders. Some of the angry warriors decided to teach the enemy a lesson that they would not soon forget. In 1852, an entire wagon train including sixty-five settlers was ambushed. Everyone in the party was killed. The settlers named the place Bloody Point. A short while later, a group of settlers pretended to want to make

The late 1800s were a difficult time for the Modoc people. Newcomers would often move in seeking to claim the territory lived on by Native Americans for thousands of years. This often led to violent and bloody conflicts.

peace. Their leader was a settler named Ben Wright. When the Native Americans arrived to begin to talk, the foreigners launched their own ambush. Forty-one unarmed Modoc were killed. It was now clear that this fight would be to the death.

Between 1853 and 1856, many of the Modoc's western neighbors tried to protect themselves in what were called the Rogue River Indian Wars. During this conflict, the miners were allowed to roam through the native lands, killing anyone they found. The army was supposed to help protect the natives who wanted peace, but it mostly helped the bloodthirsty gangs of miners. In the end, the natives were left without any property. They were forced onto reservations where they lived in a hopeless condition of poverty.

In 1864, the Modoc reluctantly agreed to move out of their homes and relocate to the Klamath Reservation in southern Oregon. When they arrived, they discovered their cousins, the Klamath, and another native nation, known as the Snakes, were already in charge of the best parts of the reservation. During the previous century, the Klamath had often fought wars against the Modoc. Neither the Modoc nor the other nations had enough food. Soon there were bitter disagreements. In 1865, the Modoc fled south to their old homeland. The United States government declared them to be renegades. The army drove the Modoc into near extermination for a second time. In 1869, the Modoc signed another peace treaty and moved back to the Klamath Reservation. Less than a year later, they headed toward their old villages for a third time. Many Modoc now believed that the only way they could survive was for the government to create a new reservation near where they had always lived.

By 1870, many of the old Modoc traditions had disappeared. Horses and firearms were now used in warfare. Most of the old styles of clothing had been replaced by new garments acquired through trade. Some Modoc had begun to use the names that white people had given them.

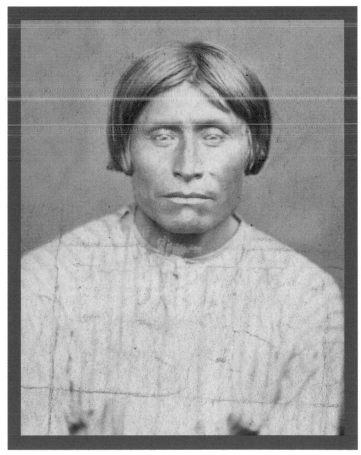

The Modoc's escape from the Klamath Reservation in 1870 proved to be a turning point in their struggle for justice. For more than a year, the army left the Native Americans alone. In 1872, the United States officially rejected Modoc demands to live at or near their old villages at Lost River. The government sent an expedition to force the people to return to the Klamath Reservation.

When the army troops showed up at the largest Modoc village, the native community leader, Kientepoos, decided to escape. He and seventy others jumped into their canoes and

Kientepoos, also known as Captain Jack, would lead his people in the Modoc War. Kientepoos's courage and bravery would inspire the Modoc to many victories against enormous odds.

began to row. As they departed the settlement, they could see the soldiers setting fire to their homes. Across the river, another group of Modoc fled their village on foot. The natives moved south with plans to join forces at the southern end of Tule Lake.

The chance to avoid a war had now been lost. Since 1870, some of the Modoc had come to believe that violence should be used to bring about the changes called for in Kientepoos's vision. Some natives supposed that if they followed the proper rituals, the army's bullets could not harm them. Kientepoos, who was known as Captain Jack to the whites, probably had a more modest objective. If they could win in the short run, the Modoc might be able to force the enemy to accept a reservation in the south. From the start, some of the natives realized the hopelessness of their situation. One group of forty-five Modoc, who had fled in 1870, decided to surrender immediately. However, before they had reached the government's outpost, a group of angry white settlers confronted them. These people said that the army was going to hang every Modoc. The forty-five natives reluctantly decided to join with the other fighters. All that seemed left was the choice of victory or death.

After they had escaped the slow-moving troops, some of the Modoc attacked nearby settlements. The natives needed food and supplies. More than a dozen of the newcomers were killed in the fighting. The deaths of these settlers ignited new hatred and fear among the whites. The government demanded that Captain Jack and his renegades be captured and punished. The army was expected to win the war quickly, as it had done in so many other struggles.

To the government's surprise, Captain Jack proved to be an excellent fighter. He knew the land, he knew his enemies, and he knew how to fight. During the months that followed, the native leader won victory after victory against overwhelming United States forces.

Kaitchkona Winema, a Modoc woman who had married a miner from Kentucky, worked as a go-between to set up the peace talks. Captain Jack explained that the Modoc wanted their own Lost River reservation and protection from the settlers. For a while, it seemed as if the war might end.

Captain Jack laid out the options to his followers. He believed that the Modoc should give up the fight and trust General

This is a portrait of Capolis, chief of the Warm Spring Indians. He helped the U.S. Army capture Captain Jack during the Modoc War.

47

Edward Canby and his soldiers. The majority of his followers did not agree. Some even questioned Captain Jack's bravery. They said that if General Canby was killed, his army would go home and the Modoc would be allowed to live wherever they wanted.

Winema heard a rumor about the plot to kill the white leader. She rode to the army camp and warned him. However, General Canby did not take her seriously. He said that she was only a foolish woman.

On April 11, 1873, the peace talks violently stopped when Captain Jack killed Canby and Reverend Eleasar Thomas. Captain

Kaitchkona Winema *(second from right)* is pictured here with her husband, Frank Riddle *(seated in chair)*, and their son, Jeff Riddle *(seated on floor)*. Winema and her husband worked as translators during the Modoc War.

Jack's followers were mistaken in their belief that if they killed Canby, the whites would give up. Instead, the government was now more determined than ever to take revenge.

It was now spring, and the weather was beginning to change. The Modoc were running out of freshwater, and they realized that they had to flee to another location. General Jefferson C. Davis was now in command of the army. He and his men were anxious to destroy all the native fighters. On April 15, 650 determined soldiers rushed into the heart of Captain Jack's stronghold. However, the natives were already gone. All the soldiers found were empty campsites.

This illustration shows the horror of the bloody Modoc War. Magazines and newspapers often unfairly depicted the Modoc as savages.

On April 26, Davis was convinced that victory was once again at hand. At a place called Hardin Butte, he ordered his men to rush forward. This time the Modoc would not escape! However, Davis and his men ran into an ambush. The defeated troops retreated. The outnumbered Modoc had less than ninety fighters. The United States had more than a thousand troops who were supported by Native American allies and an untold number of volunteers.

Although they had fought well, the Modoc were gradually realizing that they could never win the war. Some of the warriors surrendered in hopes that they could avoid punishment. Captain Jack organized

This photo, taken in 1873, shows some of the American forces during the Modoc War. After General Canby was killed, General Jefferson C. Davis (*inset*) commanded American forces for the remainder of the war.

another ambush at Sorass Lake. Unfortunately, this time, things went wrong. Several natives were killed. Worse, most of the ammunition and the supplies were captured by the army. Three hundred soldiers pushed ahead and surrounded Captain Jack and his remaining thirty-three followers at Sandy Butte. Although they were outnumbered more than ten to one, Captain Jack and his warriors escaped.

During the next month, most of Captain's Jack's men began to quarrel. Their hopes for victory became a painful memory. Little by little, the number of fighters who had surrendered grew. The army promised them they would be treated as prisoners of war. This meant that they would not be tried for killing or stealing in the white courts. On June 1, 1873, Captain Jack gave up. He handed the soldiers his rifle and became a prisoner.

The army had now spent more than half a million dollars in the Modoc War. In today's money, that meant that several billion dollars had been consumed. A total of eighty-three soldiers and settlers had been killed. By contrast, the natives lost only seventeen warriors. The dead included Canby, the only army general ever killed during the wars fought by the United States against native nations. Victory had been gained at an extremely high price.

There were 160 Modoc survivors. Nearly all of them were loaded on wagons and taken to Redding, California. From here, the natives were packed into freight cars and shipped on a railroad train to their final destination, a bleak reservation in Oklahoma. Captain Jack and seven other warriors were tried for the crime of killing Canby and Thomas during the peace talks. All of the men were found guilty. Captain Jack and four of his warriors were to be hanged. President Ulysses S. Grant changed the death sentences for two of the other natives to life in prison.

At precisely 10:20 on the morning of October 3, 1873, Captain Jack was hanged. Some of the white people were still not satisfied. Before the bodies could be buried, they removed the heads. The bloody trophies were pickled in jars of alcohol and shown at county fairs. By doing this, the natives' enemies sought to punish them even beyond the grave.

At the end of 1873, the future of the Modoc Nation seemed bleak. A small number of people had remained on the Klamath Reservation when Captain Jack left in 1870. Most of the Modoc had been exiled to Oklahoma, more than 2,000 miles (3,219 kilometers) from their traditional homeland. The invaders had taken their lands and their way of making a living. On the reservation, government agents tried to eliminate the Modoc's sense of who they were. Native children were forced into schools where they were punished for using their people's language. Native Americans were not even considered citizens. They had no legal claim to basic human rights.

The conditions at the Quapaw Indian Reservation in Oklahoma were especially bleak. While the Modoc were forced to live in crude barracks built out of wood, the government official that ruled them lived in a nearby mansion. The two structures were built close together so that he could keep an eye on the Modoc. The new environment made it hard for the natives to continue their traditions. The government gradually persuaded the Oklahoma Modoc to take up farming. Each native family grew their own crops of wheat and corn. Before 1890, many of the Modoc joined the Quaker Church (the Society of Friends).

In 1888, the Modoc Nation was given a special plot of 4,000 acres (1,619 hectares) in Oklahoma. It became the official Modoc Reservation. In 1909, the exiled natives were finally given the option of going home to the Klamath Reservation in Oregon. Some of the people did. Here they found some of their relatives living in peace with other native peoples. Most of the Modoc remained in Oklahoma. The reservation had become their home. By 1910, the surviving Modoc numbered about 300 people.

This photograph shows Modoc people during the era after the war. Most of the natives were forced onto reservations in Oregon and Oklahoma.

Five

The Modoc Today

As the new century developed, the economic conditions on both the Oklahoma and Klamath River reservations steadily improved. In 1924, all Native Americans became United States citizens. The Modoc became successful farmers, ranchers, and lumbermen. By the middle of the century, the Klamath Reservation was one of the wealthiest in the United States.

Many Washington officials felt that it was time to bring an end to the reservation system. They wanted the Native Americans to live like most other citizens. They did not understand that many natives wanted to continue their lives as part of their traditional communities. In 1954, the Klamath Reservation and the Oklahoma Modoc Reservation were dissolved by the U.S. government. The destruction of these institutions was not supported by tribal leaders. A short time after the two Modoc reservations were eliminated, the government realized that it was a bad idea and stopped the program. However, for a while it seemed as if the Modoc would not be able to reclaim their legal status as a nation.

Despite the horrors that have taken place since 1850, the Modoc spirit of resistance and courage has survived. Today, there

After many generations of bloody conflicts, the Modoc territory today can seem as beautiful and peaceful as it was in the days before Europeans moved in.

are about 200 members of the tribe who still live on reservation lands in Oklahoma. Many other individuals who have Modoc ancestors live in parts of southern Oregon and northern California. Some of the people who live in Oregon are active members of the Klamath Tribes community.

Many Modoc traditions have been lost. However, the Modoc people have not forgotten who they are. Cheewa James, a member of the nation who lives in Oklahoma, speaks and writes about

The rich history of the Modoc people is not forgotten. Here, people reenact the movement of troops during the Modoc War. The reenactment was part of the 125th anniversary of the Modoc War in 1998.

her people's history. She views the bad events of the past with a combination of understanding and compassion. Her efforts are ultimately based on her desire to create a better America and a better world. James's ideas are shared by many other Modoc. They are a people who will continue to creatively contribute to the larger story of the human experience.

This cross marks the grave of General Canby, who was killed by the Modoc in 1873. **57**

Timeline

13,000– 40,000 years ago	The ancestors of the Modoc people arrive in North America from Asia.
1540–1820	Europeans explore and begin to settle other parts of California. The Modoc do not have any direct contact with the newcomers.
1820–1840	White trappers from Washington and Oregon make occasional contact with the Modoc.
1846–1848	The United States conquers the region of California.
1849	The gold rush begins in the Sierra Nevada and later in the Mount Shasta area. The miners soon begin to kill the Native American owners of the land.
1853	First Rogue River War sees the Modoc's neighbors defeated.
1855–1856	Second Rogue River War. The Modoc's neighbors are once again defeated and sent to central Oregon.

1863	Fort Klamath is founded by the United States Army to protect settlers from Native Americans living in southern Oregon, including the Modoc.
1865	Fort Bidwell is founded by settlers. United States troops soon occupy the base. It will remain the main center for fighting against natives in northeastern California until 1893.
1872–1873	The Modoc War. The survivors of those that participated are exiled to Oklahoma.
1888	The Modoc Reservation is established in Oklahoma.
1909	The Modoc of Oklahoma are given permission to return to Oregon.
1924	All Native Americans are made U.S. citizens.
1954	The Klamath and Oklahoma Modoc Reservations are dissolved by the U.S. government.
1967	Oklahoma Modoc Reservation organizes a new tribal government.
1978	Federal government grants full recognition to Oklahoma Modoc.

Glossary

ambush (AM-bush) To attack by surprise from a hiding place.

bola (BO-la) A set of two or more stones tied to long pieces of leather that are thrown together to capture birds and small animals.

composite bow (cum-POZ-it BO) A bow made from a combination of animal muscle and wood.

cranial deformation (KRAY-nee-ull dee-for-MAY-shun) A kind of change made to the skull that causes it to change its shape.

extermination (ek-STERM-in-ay-shun) To get rid of by killing off.

pestle (PES-tuhl) Cylinder-shaped stone that is used with large rocks and baskets to grind nuts and seeds into flour.

petroglyph (PEH-truh-glif) Rock art that has designs created by scratching or carving.

pictograph (PIK-toh-graf) Rock art that has designs created using paint.

renegades (ren-EH-gaydz) People who reject lawful behavior.

reservation (reh-zer-VAY-shun) An area of land set aside by the government for Native Americans to live on.

rituals (RIH-choo-ulz) Religious ceremonies.

Resources

BOOKS

Campbell, Paul D. *Survival Skills of Native Californians.* Salt Lake City: Gibbs Smith, 1999.

Malinowski, Sharon, ed. *Gale Encyclopedia of Native American Tribes.* Detroit: Gale Group, 1998.

Rawl, James J. *Indians of California: The Changing Image.* Norman, OK: University of Oklahoma Press, 1986.

MUSEUMS AND PARKS

Lava Beds National Monument
P.O. Box 867
Tulelake, CA 96134

Modoc County Museum
600 South Main Street
Alturas, CA 96101

WEB SITES

Due to the changing nature of Internet links, the Rosen Publishing Group, Inc., has developed an online list of Web sites related to the subject of this book. This site is updated regularly. Please use this link to access the list:

http://www.rosenlinks.com/lnac/modo

Index

63